The Inca Empire

SANDRA NEWMAN

Children's Press®
An Imprint of Scholastic Inc.
New York   Toronto   London   Auckland   Sydney
Mexico City   New Delhi   Hong Kong
Danbury, Connecticut

Content Consultant

Jeremy Ravi Mumford, Ph.D.

Junior Fellow, Michigan Society of Fellows

Library of Congress Cataloging-in-Publication Data

Newman, Sandra, 1965-
   The Inca Empire / by Sandra Newman.
      p. cm. — (A true book)
   Includes index.
      ISBN-13: 978-0-531-25228-4 (lib. bdg.)   978-0-531-24109-7 (pbk.)
      ISBN-10: 0-531-25228-0 (lib. bdg.)   0-531-24109-2 (pbk.)

1. Incas—Juvenile literature. I. Title.

F3429.N484 2010

985'.019—dc22   2009000293

22 23 24 R 24 23 22 21   113

Scholastic Inc., 557 Broadway, New York, NY 10012.

Find the Truth!

Everything you are about to read is true *except* for one of the sentences on this page.

Which one is **TRUE**?

T or F The Incas were skilled builders.

T or F The Inca Empire had no emperors.

Find the answers in this book.

Ancient ceremonial mask

Contents

THE **BIG** TRUTH!

The Lost City

Machu Picchu

Almost all of the people in the Inca Empire were farmers. ➡

Ancient gold mask from Peru

Sacsayhuamán (socks-I-wah-mahn) overlooks the city of Cusco, Peru. Cusco (KOOS-ko) was the capital of the Inca Empire.

CHAPTER 1

Amazing Empire

The Incas were an amazing people. Around 1438 C.E., they formed one of the largest **empires** in South America. Without horses, or inventions like the wheel, or writing, the Incas built big cities and ruled over millions of people. They constructed thousands of miles of roads through mountains. But the Inca Empire lasted for only about 100 years!

At one time, the Inca Empire stretched more than 2,500 miles (4,023 kilometers) north to south.

Mountain Mix

The Inca Empire was originally called Tawantinsuyu (tah-wahn-tin-SOO-yoo). It was based high in the Andes mountain range of what is now the country of Peru. Tawantinsuyu had a number of different **climates** ranging from steamy jungles to the driest desert in the world, located along the coast of the Pacific Ocean.

Tawantinsuyu means "the four parts together."

Tawantinsuyu had four states, one each in the north, south, east, and west.

Colombia

Ecuador

Peru

Brazi

N
W E
S

Machu Picchu

● Cusco

Boli

Inca Empire in 1532 C.E.

Chile

Arge

KEY

Inca Empire

8

Corn, potatoes, and an herb called quinoa (KEEN-wah) were the Incas' main crops.

Breaking Ground

In the valleys among the mountain ranges, the Incas grew grains, vegetables, and fruit. Growing crops on steep mountain hillsides was not easy. The soil was not very good and there were often **droughts** (DROWTS). When it did rain, crops and soil could be washed away. Using rocks and trees, the Incas created **terraces** along the hillsides. The terraces allowed them to have flat surfaces for planting and kept their crops from sliding downhill. The Incas also built canals to bring water to their crops when it didn't rain.

9

Plants

The Incas grew 20 kinds of corn and 240 kinds of potatoes. With the temperature changes in the mountains, they were able to freeze and dry out corn and potatoes, which were then stored in warehouses. With these warehouses, the Incas were able to stock up on food to get them through a drought or if crops were ruined by freezing temperatures.

People from Europe did not know about the potato until after the Spanish visited the Inca Empire.

Inca warehouse

Llama

Animals

Animals were important to the Incas, who raised herds of llamas and alpacas for their wool. Only wealthy Incas ate llama meat. Llamas were also used for transportation. Parrots and other jungle birds were hunted for their brightly colored feathers. The feathers were used on capes worn by the royal Incas. The Incas even used guano (GWAH-no), or bird droppings, to fertilize their soil. The guano came from birds that lived on the coast. The Incas carried the guano from the coast to the high mountains.

Huayna Capac
(WHY-nah KAH-pahk)
was the Sapa Inca
in the early 1500s.

CHAPTER 2

City in the Mountains

In a valley in the Andes Mountains, the Incas founded the city of Cusco, which still exists today. Cusco was known as the capital city of the Inca Empire. It was ruled by the very powerful Sapa Inca, or emperor. The Incas believed that the emperor was a living god. His **ancestor** (AN-ses-ter) was the sun god, Inti.

Sapa Inca means "the only Inca."

Cusco is one of the highest cities in the world.

Grand and Gold

Cusco was an impressive city filled with palaces, temples, schools, and houses. The Incas built them out of stones that were carefully fit together without the use of **mortar**. The temples were decorated with gold and silver. One of the most important temples in the center of Cusco was Coricancha (co-ree-KAHN-chah) or the "Golden Courtyard." It was built to worship Inti, the sun god. Coricancha's walls were covered in sheets of pure gold and its courtyard was filled with gold and silver statues.

Pyramid of Power

The Sapa Inca had complete power over an empire of millions of people. Since this was a big job, the empire had to be well organized. Beneath the Sapa Inca were the High Priest and Army Commander-in-Chief. Next came the *apus* or lords. Each of them managed one of the four parts of the kingdom. At the bottom were the workers whose families were organized into groups called *ayllus*.

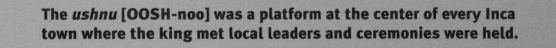

The *ushnu* [OOSH-noo] was a platform at the center of every Inca town where the king met local leaders and ceremonies were held.

Staying Connected

With such a large empire, the Incas needed to find ways to bring people together. They did this by building more than 14,000 mi. (22,530 km) of roads and hundreds of bridges that connected people across jungles, rivers, mountains, and deserts.

The roads were used by the emperor, llama herders transporting food and supplies to cities, the army, and runners who delivered messages. The runners, or *chasquis* (CHAH-skis), lived in huts placed four to six miles apart on the roads. They would run from their own hut to the next one and shout a message to another *chasqui*. Since the Incas didn't write, each *chasqui* had to learn the message by heart. Like a relay race, the message would continue to be passed until it reached its final location. A message could travel 150 mi. (241 km) in a day!

Inca roads had rest stops where travelers could spend the night and cook a meal.

Ordinary people had to be given permission to use roads like this one that still exists today.

Arts and Crafts

The Incas had great respect for artists. Inca artists made all kinds of items including necklaces of gold and seashells, and pottery. Inca men and women were also very skilled weavers. They wove robes with hundreds of little squares, each with its own design. The Incas wove wool into clothes, blankets, ropes, and baskets. Some weavers also used feathers.

Some people who live in Peru today still use the same weaving style as the ancient Incas.

Code of Knots and Colors

The emperor and his advisers needed to keep track of how many people lived throughout the huge empire and how much work they were getting done. Since they did not have a written language to record this information, the Incas used a tool called a *quipu* (KEE-poo). Quipus had a main string to which many colored strings were tied. Each string had a knot. Messengers would carry *quipus* back to the emperor, but only specially trained men could read them.

The city of Chan Chan was built by the Chimu (chee-MOO), a tribe that the Incas conquered as they were forming their empire.

CHAPTER 3

Rise to Power

Before the Inca Empire began, there were many different tribes living in the Andes Mountains. Each spoke their own language and had different **traditions**, clothes, and religious beliefs. The Incas were one of these many tribes and they were a small group. They were constantly at war with other tribes.

 At one time, the Inca Empire ruled over 86 different tribes.

The Moche and Chimu made pottery in the shapes of animals and people.

Before the Incas

Long before the Incas rose to power, two other tribes ruled Peru's northern coast and built the largest cities in Peru. One of these tribes was the Moche (MAW-chey) who lived in the Moche Valley of Northern Peru. They were great artists and builders. Their rule ended when the Chimu tribe defeated them. The Chimu created amazing **irrigation** (ir-uh-GAY-shen) systems for getting water to dry land. During their quests to take over land, the Chimu ran up against the Incas and were conquered. Some of the Chimu who survived ended up settling in Cusco where they served their new Inca rulers.

Chimu pottery

Moche pottery

Expanding the Empire

Between 1438 and 1527 C.E., different emperors expanded the Inca Empire. They did this by conquering neighboring tribes who lived beyond the city of Cusco. As the Inca emperors took control, the empire grew by thousands of miles. At one time, it stretched across what are now the countries of Peru, Bolivia, northern Argentina, Chile, and Ecuador.

Great Leader

One of the greatest Inca emperors was Pachacuti (pah-chah-COO-tee). Pachacuti's father, Viracocha (vee-rah-CO-chah) Inca, had been emperor before him. Viracocha's oldest son, Urcon (OOR-con), was supposed to take his father's place as emperor. But when the Incas faced a neighboring tribe in a battle, Urcon became scared and ran away. Pachacuti stayed and led the Incas to victory. After the battle, the Inca nobles insisted that Pachacuti should become the next emperor after his father died.

Cusco

The Power to Change

Pachacuti was a great leader who reorganized the Inca Empire. Under his rule, Cusco grew into the biggest and most beautiful city in Peru. Pachacuti had impressive new buildings and the system of roads constructed. He improved the Inca army. Pachacuti also changed the Inca religion so that people would worship Inti, the sun god.

Pachacuti means "he who remakes the world" in the Inca language of Quechua (KEH-choo-ah).

Divide and Conquer

To make the Inca Empire strong, Pachacuti first made sure that he had power over the areas around Cusco. Then he moved on to conquer regions far beyond the city. Pachacuti felt it was very important to build an empire in which everyone worked together and spoke the same language. He did not kill the people whose land he conquered. Instead, he and his advisers would invite them to join the Inca Empire. If people refused, the Inca army would force them to give up.

All in the Family

In 1471 C.E., Pachacuti's son, Topa Yupanqui (TOE-pah yoo-PANK-ee), became the next Sapa Inca. He was a great general who continued his father's conquests. Of all the Inca rulers, Topa Yupanqui was the emperor who added the most land to the Inca Empire. Under his rule, the empire covered more than 2,000 mi. (3,218 km) of the Andes Mountains, the Amazon jungle, and the coast. Topa's son, Huayna Capac, took over the empire at the end of his father's rule.

The Inca army carried drums, flutes, and trumpets into battle.

The Lost City

Machu Picchu (MA-choo PEEK-choo) or "Old Peak" has been called "The Lost City of the Incas." It is located more than 7,000 feet (2,133 meters) above sea level at the top of a mountain outside of Cusco. Experts believe that Pachacuti built Machu Picchu around 1460 C.E., as a country estate or royal retreat.

Sun Stone

The Intihuatana [in-tee-wa-TA-na] Stone or "hitching post to the sun" was one of the most important discoveries at Machu Picchu. It is believed that as the winter solstice was to begin, a priest would hold a ceremony to tie the sun to the stone. The Incas thought this would keep the sun from disappearing.

Building Blocks

Machu Picchu has 200 buildings that were made using perfectly cut stones. These were fitted together without mortar.

Francisco Pizarro and his men fighting the Incas

CHAPTER 4

The Fall of the Incas

In 1532 C.E., a small group of Spanish explorers arrived in Peru. They were led by Francisco Pizarro (fran-SIS-co pee-SAH-row). Pizarro and his men conquered some of the people that the Incas had already ruled over. From these people, Pizarro heard stories about the Incas and their amazing cities of gold, high in the Andes. The promise of gold excited Pizarro and so he got permission from the King of Spain to find and conquer the Inca Empire.

← Before Pizarro arrived, the Incas had never seen horses.

A Time of War

Before Pizarro arrived, a war was taking place between the two sons of Huayna Capac. Huayna Capac had died before choosing which son would become the next Sapa Inca. The sons, Huascar (WAH-scar) and Atahualpa (AT-wal-pah), both wanted to take over for their father. Each of the brothers decided to make himself the Sapa Inca and they went to war against each other.

Huascar

32

Atahualpa

For five years, the brothers and their armies fought each other to become the next emperor. In the end, Atahualpa won the war. By the time Pizarro met Atahualpa, the Inca Empire was not as strong as it had once been. Many lives had been lost both in the war and to diseases that had been spread by other explorers from Europe.

End of a Journey

On his journey to Cusco to officially become the next Sapa Inca, Atahualpa and thousands of warrior soldiers stayed in the city of Cajamarca (cah-hah-MAR-cah). Pizarro traveled there in search of the new emperor and hid men, horses, and weapons in buildings surrounding a big, empty space in the town's center. When Atahualpa and his soldiers arrived, Pizarro and his men attacked them. They captured the emperor and killed thousands of Incas.

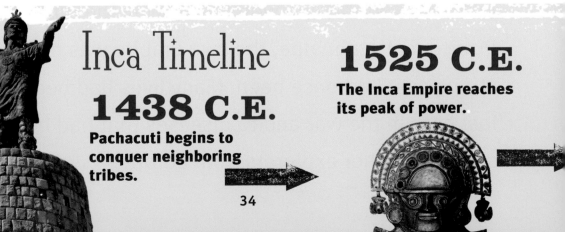

Inca Timeline

1438 C.E.
Pachacuti begins to conquer neighboring tribes.

1525 C.E.
The Inca Empire reaches its peak of power.

Pizarro brought only 167 men with him.

The Spanish said they would only release Atahualpa if the Incas gave them gold and silver. The Incas agreed and offered to fill rooms with gold and silver in exchange for Atahualpa's freedom. Over several months, they filled the rooms but in the end, Pizarro had Atahualpa killed.

1532 C.E.
Pizarro takes the Sapa Inca captive. Peru becomes a colony of Spain.

1824
Peru wins its independence from Spain.

Take Over

Pizarro's conquest of the Incas continued and finally he reached Cusco. Once he was there, Pizarro made one of Atahualpa's brothers, Manco (MAN-koh) Inca, the next Sapa Inca. At first, Manco Inca cooperated but then he fought the Spanish. Even though the Incas had many troops and the Spanish had very few, the Incas eventually lost the war. Manco Inca left Cusco and settled in a valley where he oversaw an Inca state until his death in 1544 C.E. The Spanish captured and killed the last Inca leader in 1572 C.E. Once the Spanish took over, the Inca Empire eventually disappeared.

Manco Inca

Inca Mummies

When a ruler died, the Incas wrapped the body in cloth to preserve him forever as a mummy. Each mummy would stay in the palace where the ruler had lived. During festivals, mummies were displayed for all to see. The mummies were treated like living people. Family members would visit them for advice. Food and drink were brought to the mummies as if they were still alive.

When the Spanish conquered the Incas, they destroyed the mummies of their rulers.

An archaeologist
studies bones found
in Tupac Amaru, Peru.

CHAPTER 5

The Mysterious Incas

Learning about the Incas' history has been like putting together a big puzzle. The Incas did not have a written language that provided a record of who they were and how they lived. Instead, the Incas passed down their history in words. **Archaeologists** (ahr-kee-OL-uh-jests) have been putting the puzzle pieces together by studying the architecture and **artifacts** that were left behind.

← More than 120 Inca mummies have been found at Tupac Amaru, Peru.

Ruins of ancient temple outside of Cusco

New Discoveries

Even today, archaeologists are still making discoveries about Inca history. In 2008, they found the ruins of an ancient temple outside of Cusco. It is believed that the temple was built before the Inca Empire began but that it was expanded during the time of the empire. Tourists from all over the world visit Cusco and Machu Picchu every year. Though the Inca Empire ended more than 500 years ago, people are still fascinated by the mysteries left behind.

Llamas are members of the camel family.

Machu Picchu

Visions of the Past

Throughout the country of Peru today, there are signs of the way the ancient Incas lived. In some villages, the Inca language of Quechua is still spoken. People in some parts of the country still use llamas to carry things and they raise them for their wool. Some artists in Peru still weave just as the Incas did before them in what was once part of the great and mysterious Inca Empire. ★

A Quechua woman weaves llama wool at a market in Peru.

True Statistics

Number of people ruled by the Incas when the Spanish came: About 12 million

Number of years the Inca Empire lasted: Nearly 100 years

Number of kinds of potatoes grown by the Incas: 240

Height of Machu Picchu: More than 7,000 ft. (2,133 m) above sea level

Size of Inca Empire: 2,500 mi. (4,023 km), north to south

Total length of the roads built by the Incas: 14,000 mi. (22,530 km)

Distance traveled by the Inca mail: 150 mi. (241 km) a day

Monument to Pachacuti in Cusco, Peru

Did you find the truth?

(T) The Incas were skilled builders.

(F) The Inca Empire had no emperors.

Resources

Books

Bingham, Jane. *The Inca Empire* (Time Travel Guides). Chicago: Raintree, 2007.

Braman, Arlette. *The Incas: Activities and Crafts from a Mysterious Land* (Secrets of Ancient Cultures). Hoboken, NJ: Wiley, 2004.

Conklin, Wendy. *Mayas, Aztecs, Incas.* New York: Scholastic, 2006.

Deary, Terry. *Incredible Incas Activity Book.* New York: Scholastic, 2005.

Deary, Terry. *The Angry Aztecs and the Incredible Incas.* New York: Scholastic, 2004.

Drew, David. *Inca Life* (Life of Early Civilization). Irvine, CA: Saddleback Educational Publishing, 2006.

Lewin, Ted. *Lost City: The Discovery of Machu Picchu.* New York: Philomel Books, 2003.

Saunders, Nicholas. *Pizarro and the Incas* (Stories from History). Grand Rapids, MI: School Specialty Publishing, 2006.

White, Laurie J. *Baktar: A Tale from the Andes.* Covington, GA: Shorter Word Press, 2007.

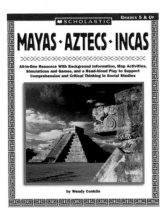

Organizations and Web Sites

About the Incas
http://library.thinkquest.org/5058/inca.htm
Visit this site to read more about the history, religion, and culture of the Incas.

The Incredible Incas for Kids
http://incas.mrdonn.org
Take a trip through the history of the Inca Empire at this site.

Descendants of the Incas
www.incas.org
Check out this Web site to find out about how Inca people are living near Cusco today.

Places to Visit

The Field Museum
1400 S. Lake Shore Drive
Chicago, IL 60605-2496
(312) 922-9410
www.fieldmuseum.org/
ancientamericas
Visit the Ancient Americas exhibition and learn about the Inca Empire builders.

Brooklyn Museum
200 Eastern Parkway
Brooklyn, NY 11238-6052
(718) 638-5000
www.brooklynmuseum.org
View portraits of Inca kings and Inca objects.

Important Words

ancestor (AN-ses-ter) – a person from whom one is descended and who lived generations ago

archaeologists (ahr-kee-OL-uh-jests) – scientists who study history by looking at artifacts

artifacts – objects that were made by people, such as tools or weapons

climates – the normal weather conditions of a region

droughts (DROWTS) – long periods with little or no rain

empires – groups of people or countries under the control of one ruler

irrigation (ir-uh-GAY-shen) – a man-made way of getting water to land

mortar – a mixture like cement, used to hold bricks or stones in place

retreat – a quiet place where people go to rest or be alone

solstice – the two times of year (in December and June) when the sun is farthest from the equator

terraces – flat, raised sections of ground

traditions – beliefs or customs that are passed down from people over many years

Index

Page numbers in **bold** indicate illustrations

About the Author

Sandra Newman writes fiction and nonfiction books for both children and adults. She also teaches writing and translates books from foreign languages. She has traveled in Peru and Bolivia, lands that were formerly part of ancient *Tawantinsuyu*.

PHOTOGRAPHS © 2010: BigStockPhoto (©Alexey Stiop, p. 4; p. 14; ©Chris Howey, p. 20; Pachacuti, p. 34; p. 43; ©Gino Santa Maria, Peru flag, p. 35; ©Matt Trommer, p. 14; ©Paul Clarke, p. 10; ©Sergio Assini, p. 37); Dreamstime (p. 3); Getty Images (p. 26; Intihuatana Stone, p. 29; p. 38); iStockphoto (©Carlos Santa Maria, gold mask, p. 5; ©Jarno Gonzalez, p. 9; ©Roger Van Bulck, statue of Pizarro, p. 35); Photolibrary (back cover; p. 12; pp. 17–18; pp. 23–25; Machu Picchu, pp. 28-29; p. 32; gold mask, p. 34; Pizarro meeting Atahualpa, p. 35; p. 36; pp. 41–42;); photonewzealand/topfoto (p. 19); Tranz (Corbis: cover; Inca farming, p. 5; p. 6; p. 15; p. 30; p. 33; Reuters: p. 40)